KV-514-349

TESTING AND ASSESSMENT IN THE NATIONAL CURRICULUM

Pupils between the ages of 7 and 11 (Years 3–6) cover Key Stage 2 of the National Curriculum. In May of their final year of Key Stage 2 (Year 6), all pupils take written National Tests (commonly known as SATs) in three core subjects: English, Maths and Science. Your child should already have taken some National Tests at the end of Key Stage 1 (Year 2) in Maths (number, shape and space), English Reading and English Writing.

At the end of Key Stage 1, children are awarded a National Curriculum level for each subject tested. When children eventually take Key Stage 2 tests, they are again awarded a level. On average, pupils are expected to advance one level for every two years they are at school. The target for pupils at the end of Key Stage 1 is Level 2. By the end of Key Stage 2, four years later, the target is Level 4. The table below shows the average target levels.

	7 years	11 years
Exceptional performance — Level 6		■
Level 5		■
Exceeded targets for age group — Level 4	■	■
Achieved targets for age group — Level 3	■	□
Level 2	■	□
Working towards targets for age group — Level 1	□	□

IMPROVING YOUR CHILD'S UNDERSTANDING AT KEY STAGE 2

This series will help you to work with your child to improve his or her knowledge and understanding of English, Maths and Science throughout Key Stage 2. There are four books for each subject – one for each year, starting with 7–8 year-olds. The activities in the books are appropriate to the target levels for each year and to the topics your child may study during that year.

These books may be used in conjunction with Letts' Progress Test books, also in the *At Home With The National Curriculum* range. The Progress books provide test materials to assess your child's level of knowledge at each year of Key Stage 2 and so tell you the areas in which he or she needs most help.

HOW TO USE THIS BOOK

The work in this book is at Levels 4–5 and is appropriate for the average 10–11 year-old. This book contains the following features:

Eleven four-page Units (pages 3–46) each incorporating:

- Notes to parents, explaining the relevance of the topic to the National Curriculum, a description of the activity and helpful 'Teaching points' advising you how to tackle common areas of difficulty.

- Two colourful information and activity pages for your child to work through with your help or on his or her own.

- Further questions and activities related to the topic, accompanied by more ideas for helping your child to understand the subject.

The topics covered in this book, and their page numbers, are as follows:

There is an Answers section at the back of the book.

Working through this book with your child

- Your child should not attempt to do all the activities in the book in one go. Work through each topic Unit together, allowing plenty of time for discussion and explanation of the subject. Encourage your child to attempt as many of the activities as possible without help, then use the further activities and ideas to expand on the subject. Do not move on to the next Unit until your child fully understands the one he or she is working on.

- Where children are asked to boil water or use sharp implements this warning symbol appears in the text: ⚠ ADULT HELP NEEDED

- The Answers section at the back of the book provides answers where possible. Check these with your child when each activity has been completed and discuss his or her findings. For some of the activities the answers depend on your child's results or predictions. You will have to judge the appropriateness of your child's answers.

- If your child has difficulty understanding a particular topic, the 'More ways to help your child' section offers methods of explaining a subject in less formal situations.

Equipment your child will need

The following may be needed for answering the questions in this book:

- a pen or pencil for writing, a pencil for drawing, a rubber and coloured pencils;
- a ruler;
- spare paper.

Individual topic Units sometimes require additional simple equipment. Make sure you have everything your child needs before beginning each Unit.

Pumping blood

Introduction:

The heart works as a pump to send blood around the body, which needs oxygen to survive. Arteries carry blood from the heart; veins carry blood back to the heart. Most arteries carry blood rich in oxygen, while most veins carry blood that has lost its oxygen. When we exercise the heart has to pump faster and our heartbeat, shown by the pulse rate, increases. It decreases when we rest.

The heart is divided into a left side and a right side (the right side of the heart is not as you look at it but how it appears in the body). Each side has two chambers, the upper atrium and the lower ventricle. The thick outside wall of the heart is composed of muscle which regularly contracts to pump blood out of the lower chambers to the lungs and round the body. The heart is roughly in the centre of the chest and in an adult beats about 70 times a minute; a bird's heartbeat is about 500 per minute; that of the largest animals, such as elephants, is about 20.

National Curriculum:

Attainment Target 2: Life Processes and Living Things

The National Curriculum at Key Stage 2 states that children should be taught:

> *a simple model of the structure of the heart and how it acts as a pump;*
> *how blood circulates in the body through arteries and veins;*
> *and about the effect of exercise and rest on the pulse rate.*

At Level 4 children should be able to use scientific names for the major organs of the body and recognise that the heart is part of the circulatory system. At Level 5 they should be able to explain the function of the heart, arteries, veins and capillaries.

Activity:

The first activities ask children to read about the function of the heart and then complete a number of sentences related to the topic. The third activity asks children to find out what happens to their pulse rate when they take exercise and how long it takes to return to normal. Children should be encouraged to take their pulse rates several times and work out the average. The activities on the 'Now try these' page ask them to identify the arteries and veins in the body as well as some of the major organs.

Teaching points:

Explain to your child that the heart works as a pump. Show him or her other pumps, such as those used for cycle tyres or in fish tanks.

Discuss why the heart needs to pump blood around the body – what is it in the blood that needs to be transported? – and how the blood is carried.

Discuss the basic structure of the heart with its right and left sides divided into two chambers. Get your child to draw a diagram of the heart and use arrows to show how it works. Discuss what is happening when your child feels his or her pulse.

Write down some of the scientific words used and ask your child to explain what they mean.

Pumping blood

Your heart is a muscle which pumps blood around your body.

1 ───────────

Put your hand on the left side of your chest. The throbbing you can feel is your heart beating.

Blood is carried from the heart through your **arteries** and is returned to the heart through your **veins**.

The heart is split into four parts, called **chambers**. The top two are known as the **atria** and the bottom two as the **ventricles**. An adult heart weighs around 300g and is the size of a clenched fist.

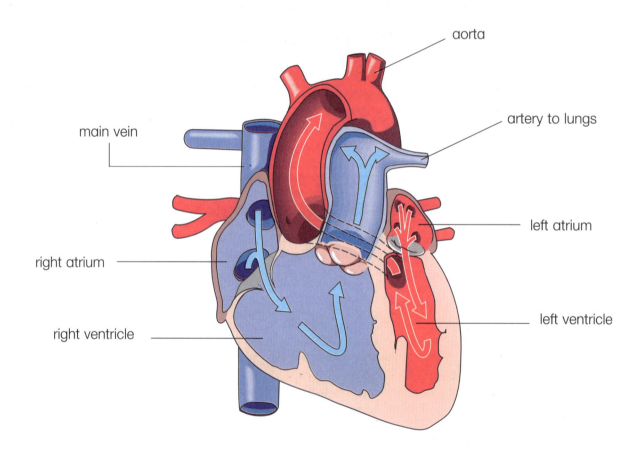

main vein

right atrium

right ventricle

aorta

artery to lungs

left atrium

left ventricle

How the heart works

Blood arrives at the heart from veins in the body.

It enters the right atrium then goes down into the right ventricle. From here it is pumped to the lungs where it collects oxygen. The whole body needs oxygen to stay alive.

The blood then enters the left atrium and flows into the left ventricle.

From here it is pumped out through the **aorta**, the main artery. Blood is carried around the rest of the body through more arteries.

2

Can you underline the right words to complete these sentences?

a Blood is carried to your heart through your (bones, arteries, veins, muscles) and away from it through your (bones, arteries, veins, muscles).

b The heart is made of (two, three, four) chambers.

c An adult heart weighs about (250g, 300g, 500g).

d Blood collects oxygen from the (lungs, heart, head, kidneys).

e The adult heart is about the size of a (football, pea, fist, tennis ball).

3

Pulse rate

Put a finger on the inside of your wrist. Can you feel a slight movement? This is your pulse, which matches the beating of your heart. It is produced by blood passing through an artery.

Using a stop-watch or the second hand of a clock, count the number of times your pulse beats in one minute. This is your pulse rate.

Take your pulse rate after doing each of the activities below, one after the other, and fill in the chart.

Activity	Pulse rate
Standing still	
Running around for 5 minutes	
Standing for 2 minutes	
Standing still for 5 minutes	

How long does it take your pulse rate to return to normal?

....

Now turn over ➤

Now try these ...

The heart pumps blood and oxygen through the arteries. From the smallest arteries, the blood goes into tiny blood vessels called **capillaries**, which pass food and oxygen into every part of the body. The capillaries also collect waste from the body. This is sent into the smallest veins which return the blood in larger veins to the heart. It then goes to the lungs to collect more oxygen, and the cycle begins again.

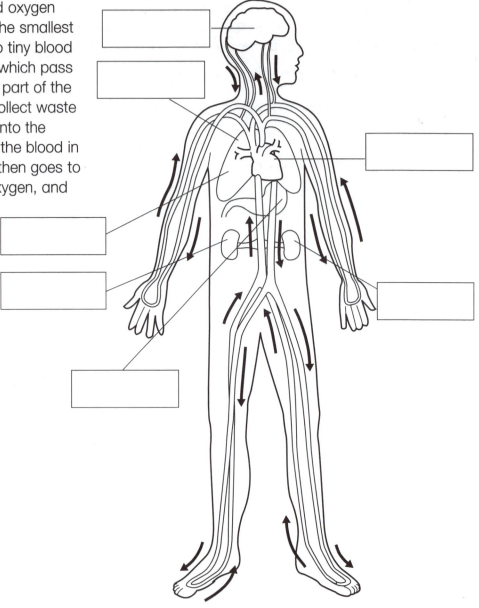

1 On the body, colour the arteries red and the veins blue. Remember, each part of the body must have an artery to supply blood and a vein to carry it away.

2 Can you label the organs on the body? Choose from this list:

heart	lung	kidney	brain	stomach

More ways to help your child:

Discuss what happens when you cut your finger. Where does the blood come from?

Break down

Introduction:

Micro-organisms are single-celled creatures found everywhere yet invisible to the naked eye. There are several types, including bacteria and viruses. Some bacteria are harmless, such as those found in yoghurt, but others can cause septic cuts and food poisoning. Bacteria also live in the soil where they help to break down dead material. Bacterial diseases, such as typhoid and diphtheria, often flourish in poor-quality water or may be spread by water-borne bacteria released into the air when people cough or sneeze. Viruses cause many diseases in animals and humans such as the common cold and chicken pox. The average size of a virus is about 50 millionths of a millimetre across.

National Curriculum:

Attainment Target 2: Life Processes and Living Things

At Key Stage 2 children should be taught:

*that micro-organisms exist, and that many may be beneficial,
for example in the breakdown of waste, whilst others may be harmful,
for example in causing disease.*

At Level 4 children should have an increasing awareness of the range of living things and that living things depend on each other to survive. At Level 5 children should recognise that there is a great variety of living things and understand the importance of classification. They should be able to explain why different organisms are found in different habitats.

Activity:

The first activity involves making yoghurt using a live culture. (Live yoghurt should be available from your local supermarket.) The second activity asks children to make a Tulgren Funnel, a simple piece of apparatus used to separate minibeasts from leaf litter. After an hour, there should be a number of creatures, such as woodlice and millipedes, in the bottom of the jar. These creatures live in damp, wet places and so move away from the light and heat of the desk lamp and fall through the funnel into the glass jar. Always encourage children to return creatures they have studied to their natural habitat. The activity on the 'Now try these' page explores what happens when you make a compost heap. You can use various types of organic matter, including straw and grass cuttings, but do not use leftover scraps of meat etc. Any large items should be chopped up.

Teaching points:

When handling compost, your child must wear gloves. Your child could use a magnifying glass to examine the compost and to examine leaf litter.

Keep the compost damp and turn it regularly. It should become crumbly as it begins to decompose. Handle the worms carefully and put them back after a few days at the most.

Explain to your child that there are other micro-organisms apart from bacteria, such as viruses which can cause flu and colds, and that some bacteria infect cuts and cause stomach upsets. Discuss the ways in which micro-organisms may be carried in the air or water and passed on from one person to another.

Break down

Bacteria are very small living creatures. Some can cause diseases, but others are helpful.

1

Making yoghurt

You will need:

a pan
a Thermos flask or large screw-top jar
500ml full-fat, long-life milk
a tablespoon of live yoghurt

ADULT HELP
NEEDED

1 Pour the milk into the pan. Ask an adult to heat it slowly, without letting it boil.

2 Pour the milk into the flask or jar until almost full up.

3 Add the live yoghurt to the milk and stir the mixture.

4 Seal the flask or jar and leave it to stand. If you use a jar, put it somewhere warm, such as an airing cupboard.

After several days, unscrew the top and you will have a container full of yoghurt. You may like to add a flavouring such as jam to your yoghurt before you eat it.

The live yoghurt contains harmless bacteria. These work on the milk and turn it into yoghurt. Most bacteria like warm, moist conditions where they can grow.

Bacteria are so small they can only be seen under a microscope.

2 —————————

Bacteria can also be useful for breaking down waste, known as **decomposition**. Other creatures and micro-organisms work with bacteria to decompose waste. These include minibeasts such as earthworms and millipedes, which feed on dead plants.

You can find these minibeasts in the leaf litter of a compost heap.

You will need:

a desk lamp
a handful of damp, dead leaves
a large, see-through jar
a plastic funnel
tissues
black paper
sticky tape

1 Put damp tissues into the bottom of the large jar and cover it with black paper.

2 Fill the funnel with leaves and place it over the jar.

3 Shine the light onto the leaves for an hour. What do you collect in your jar? Use a magnifying glass and a field guide to identify the creatures. Do you know why these creatures have fallen into the jar?

You might like to record your observations on a separate piece of paper.

Remember to put the creatures back where you found them.

Now turn over ➤

Now try these ...

When leaves and other plant remains break down they make compost.
Compost is full of the vital nutrients that living plants need to grow. It is made by bacteria and other creatures breaking down dead material.

Make your own compost heap

You will need:

ADULT HELP
NEEDED

a small wooden box
torn-up newspaper or leaves
a few earthworms
kitchen waste, such as tea leaves or vegetable peelings
(do not use any leftover scraps of meat or other animal products)

1   Ask an adult to make some holes in the bottom of the box.

2   Put a layer of newspaper or leaves into the bottom.

3   Put several layers of kitchen waste on top. Put in the earthworms. Add more waste.

4   Wait for a couple of days, keeping the mixture somewhere cool and dark. Add more waste if necessary.

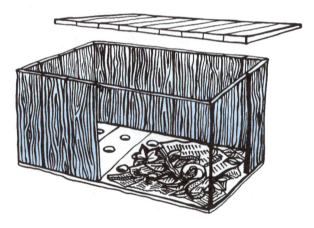

The worms and the bacteria in the air will break the waste down.

What happens to the waste? What does it look like?

More ways to help your child:

Bury objects made of various materials, such as a plastic bag, a newspaper and a tin can, in the garden or in several large flower pots. Examine them after two weeks to see what has happened. Discuss the environmental implications of each type of material.

A third type of micro-organism is very small fungi. These also help to break down dead material. Look for fungi growing on tree stumps where they feed off rotting wood. Fungi can also cause disease, for example athlete's foot. Making bread with yeast, a minute fungus, is another way to show how useful some micro-organisms can be.

Shadow time

Introduction:

As the Earth spins on its axis one complete rotation every 24 hours, the Sun appears to move across the sky from east to west and we have night and day. With a shadow stick it is possible to track the path of the Sun and show that it is at its highest at midday, when the shadow is shortest. The Earth's axis is tilted so there are considerable differences between shadows in winter and summer, when the Sun is much higher in the sky.

The Earth also orbits the Sun as it spins, taking just over 365 days to complete one orbit. Similarly the Moon takes about one month (28 days) to orbit the Earth. Half of the Moon is always lit by the Sun. As it orbits the Earth we can see different amounts of this lit surface, so making the Moon appear to change shape from a crescent to a circle then back to a crescent.

National Curriculum:

Attainment Target 4: Physical Processes

At Key Stage 2 children are taught that:

> *the position of the Sun appears to change during the day, and how
> shadows change as this happens; that the Earth orbits the Sun once a
> year and the Moon takes approximately 28 days to orbit the Earth.*

At Level 4 children should use the idea that light travels in straight lines to explain phenomena such as the formation of shadows and how the position of the Sun changes over the course of a day. At Level 5 children should be able to use models to explain effects caused by the movement of the Earth, such as the length of a day or year.

Activity:

The first activity looks at how shadows change in length as the Sun moves across the sky. It is the Earth spinning on its axis that makes the Sun appear to move. Shadows shorten and lengthen according to the height of the Sun above the horizon. The second activity then asks children to make a simple shadow clock. The third activity looks at the Earth in space. Children are asked to compare the sizes of the Earth and the Sun using objects such as a beach ball and a table tennis ball. (Emphasise that these are only approximate comparisons.) The follow-up activities on the 'Now try these' page look at how the Earth orbits the Sun while the Moon orbits the Earth. This is then followed by a study of the Moon to see how its shape appears to change in a regular cycle.

Teaching points:

Your child must never look directly at the Sun, as this can permanently damage the eyes.

To make the shadow stick give your child a stick about 30cm long, and a good-sized piece of Plasticine or a small container of sand. Make sure that the stick is placed in a sunny spot on a flat surface, away from trees that may produce other shadows. Emphasise that your child should not move the stick.

Children often confuse the Earth's spin on its axis with its movement around the Sun. Making models with a football and a tennis ball or using a ball and a table lamp can help your child's understanding.

Shadow time

The Earth spins round on its axis once every 24 hours. As it spins, the Sun appears to travel across the sky. Since ancient times, people have told the time by measuring the position of the Sun.

1

Make a shadow stick

You will need:

a stick about 30cm long
a large piece of Plasticine or a tub of sand

⚠ NEVER LOOK DIRECTLY AT THE SUN – YOU COULD DAMAGE YOUR EYES.

Push the stick into the sand or Plasticine.
Place it outside, on flat ground away from trees, on a sunny day.

Look at your stick at different times of the day. On the drawings below, mark the position of the Sun and the shadow at the following times:

a early morning **b** midday **c** evening

When is the shadow shortest?...

2

Make a shadow clock

Place your shadow stick outside in the middle of a large piece of white paper. Every hour, mark the position of the shadow and write the time next to the mark.

You can now tell the time by looking at the position of the shadow. Clocks such as the one you have made were first used by the ancient Eygptians.

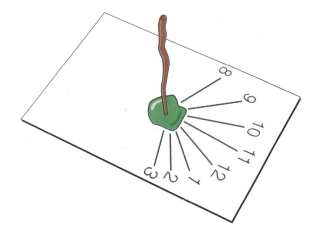

3

Earth in Space

The Earth **orbits**, or travels around, the Sun. The Sun is a star which is many times bigger than Earth. It provides us with heat and light and without it we could not survive. It takes just over 365 days (one year) for the Earth to travel once around the Sun.

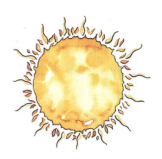

Find a beach ball (the Sun) and a table tennis ball (the Earth). Compare their sizes. If the Sun was the beach ball and the Earth the table tennis ball they would be about 10 metres away from each other.

Now turn over ➤

Now try these ...

1 At the same time as the Earth orbits the Sun, the Moon orbits the Earth.
The Moon takes 28 days to travel around the Earth once.

Ask a friend or an adult to hold a beach ball and pretend it is the Sun. Hold a table tennis ball (Earth) in one hand and a pea (Moon) in the other and walk around your friend. As you walk, move the pea around the table tennis ball. Remember that the Earth and Moon both spin while they travel.

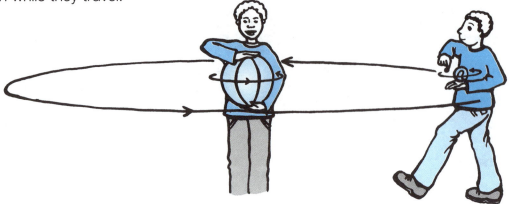

2 As the Moon orbits the Earth, it seems to change shape as we can see more and more of the half that is lit by the Sun. These are called the phases of the Moon.

New Moon
completely dark

Crescent
a thin strip is lit up

First Quarter
half the surface is lit up

Gibbous
most of the surface
is lit but not all

Full Moon
the whole of the
Moon is lit up

Gibbous
the lit portion
starts to get smaller

Last Quarter
half the Moon is visible

Crescent
a thin strip is lit up

Make a Moon diary
Observe the Moon over a month. Record its phases from New Moon to Full Moon and back again in a notebook. Don't forget to write the date beside each picture.

More ways to help your child:

Find out about the planets in the Solar System. How many are there? Which planet is nearest to the Sun? Which is furthest from the Sun? Visit a planetarium.

You should be able to see Venus in the evening. It is known as the 'evening star' even though it is a planet. It is the first object visible at night and the last to dim in the morning.

Sorting out

Introduction:

There are millions of plants and animals so scientists need a way of classifying them (arranging them into groups) in order to refer to them easily. Natural systems of classification, such as the number of legs an animal has or how the parts of its body are arranged, are used to group animals with similar structures. Animals and plants with parts arranged in the same way are generally closely related. At Key Stage 2 children start to use simple keys to identify and group animals and plants and start to recognise the importance of systematically classifying living things.

National Curriculum:

Attainment Target 2: Life Processes and Living Things

At Key Stage 2 children are taught:

how locally occurring animals and plants can be identified and assigned to groups using keys.

At Level 4 children use keys based on observable external features to help them identify and group living things systematically. At Level 5 they should recognise that there is a great variety of living things and understand the importance of classification.

Activity:

The first two activities ask children to use keys to sort out a number of animals. Children can go on to construct similar keys using different animals or plants from an area they have studied themselves, such as a pond. The next activity is based on a lateral key which uses comparison. Once a set of characteristics has been identified, it is possible to fit each creature into a group or set. Through this sort of activity, children should begin to understand the principles on which classification systems are built. The follow-on activities on the 'Now try these' page look at some of the differences between mammals, reptiles and birds.

Teaching points:

If your child wants to construct his or her own keys, start with simple examples and easily identifiable characteristics such as the number of legs a creature has, or whether or not a plant has flowers.

Your child may try to guess the name of the animal by just looking at the picture. Encourage your child to follow the key.

Look at ways in which animals are adapted to their environments. For example, ducks have shovel-shaped beaks and webbed feet.

Encourage your child to group animals together using easily recognisable features. For example: insects are the group of animals with six legs and three parts to their bodies; spiders are the group which have eight legs and two parts to their bodies.

Sorting out

Using keys, you can work out the names of most plants or animals.

1

Here are some animals you might find on the seashore.
Use the key to find out what they are. Write the correct name under each animal.

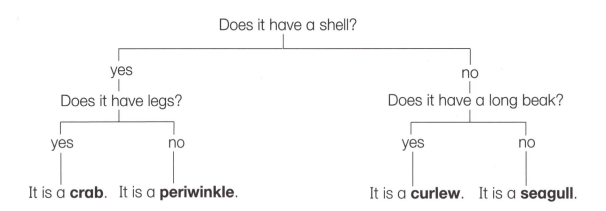

a   b   c   d

....

Does it have a shell?

yes   no

Does it have legs?   Does it have a long beak?

yes   no   yes   no

It is a **crab**.   It is a **periwinkle**.   It is a **curlew**.   It is a **seagull**.

2

On the next page is a key for minibeasts. Can you fit the names of the creatures below into the right boxes in the key?

ladybird   spider   woodlouse   worm

butterfly   snail   fly

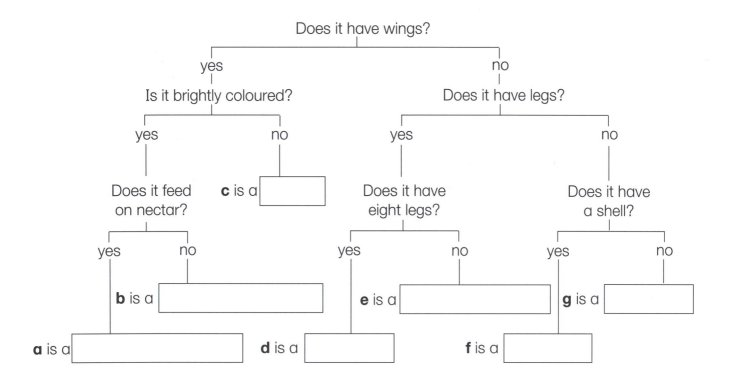

Does it have wings?

yes — Is it brightly coloured?

no — Does it have legs?

Is it brightly coloured?
yes — Does it feed on nectar?
no — **c** is a ▭

Does it have legs?
yes — Does it have eight legs?
no — Does it have a shell?

Does it feed on nectar?
yes
no — **b** is a ▭

Does it have eight legs?
yes — **e** is a ▭
no

Does it have a shell?
yes — **g** is a ▭
no

a is a ▭

d is a ▭

f is a ▭

3

Fill in this table by ticking the right boxes for each creature.

Creature	Wings	Legs	Fins	Beak	Teeth	Feathers	Hair
Salmon							
Eagle							
Dog							
Horse							
Duck							
Parrot							
Trout							
Cat							

Use a separate sheet of paper for the following activity.

Which creatures in the table share some of the same characteristics? Put them into groups. Try to make up a key like those in questions 1 and 2 to help other people identify these animals.

Now turn over ➤

Now try these ...

Here are some animal facts.

Cold-blooded animals need heat from the Sun to keep warm.
Warm-blooded animals use energy from the food they eat to keep warm.
Mammals are warm-blooded and all have hair. They give birth to live young and feed them on milk.
Reptiles are cold-blooded and have a dry, scaly skin. They lay eggs.
Birds are covered in feathers. They have wings, a beak and no teeth. Most birds can fly. Birds are warm-blooded and lay eggs.

1 What are the differences between these creatures?

a

dog

....
....
....

b

lizard

....
....
....

c

thrush

....
....
....

2 Sort these creatures into mammals (**M**), reptiles (**R**) and birds (**B**) by writing the correct letter in each box.

alligator	☐	lion	☐	crocodile	☐	ostrich	☐
horse	☐	turtle	☐	parrot	☐	albatross	☐
snake	☐	eagle	☐	bat	☐	rabbit	☐

More ways to help your child:

Visit different locations (such as a grassy area, a pond or wooded area) at different times of the day and year to see any differences that can be found. For example, lots of insects appear on warm sunny days; birds search for berries in the autumn. This will help your child to realise that living things respond to daily and seasonal changes.

Separating mixtures

Introduction:

Mixtures can be separated by a variety of methods, including sieving, filtering and evaporation. To separate solid particles from a liquid we use a sieve, or a filter for smaller particles. To separate soluble substances, such as sugar or salt, from water we would use evaporation. Materials that will not dissolve, even if they are heated or stirred, are known as insoluble.

National Curriculum:

Attainment Target 3: Materials and their Properties

At Key Stage 2 children are taught:

that some solids dissolve in water to give solutions but some do not;
and that solids that have been dissolved can be recovered by evaporating
the liquid from the solution.

At Level 4 children should be able to describe some methods used to separate simple mixtures, such as filtration, and use scientific terms to describe changes, such as evaporation and condensation. At Level 5 children should use their knowledge about how a specific mixture can be separated to suggest ways in which other similar mixtures might be separated.

Activity:

The first activity asks children to make up a mixture of different solids with a liquid. Discuss the properties of each solid and encourage children to predict the results before the mixture is made. The different processes that are needed to separate the elements are then examined. The next activity asks children to choose the best methods of separating certain mixtures. (Children could try these out for themselves.) The third activity concentrates on evaporation by asking children to examine two different mixtures: sand and water and sugar and water. It is important to point out that the sand and water stay separate and will not produce a solution. The substances can be separated by using a filter. The second example produces a solution which can be separated by evaporation.

The follow-up activities on the 'Now try these' page look at chromatography, a technique used for separating small amounts of substances from a mixture. The different substances in the mixture are absorbed at different rates, each forming a distinct layer. As colours are usually made up of more than one dye, chromatography can be used to separate the different colours in felt tip pens and food dye. Water soluble felt tip pens, rather than permanent marker pens, must be used.

Teaching points:

Your child should record and explain each stage of the experiments.

Make up some more mixtures for your child to examine and discuss how methods such as evaporation might be used in industry, for example by removing sea-salt from water. Discuss the everyday uses of separation, such as a tea bag or strainer that stops tea leaves from getting into the cup.

Encourage your child to use scientific terms such as solid, liquid, dissolves, solution and evaporate.

Separating mixtures

You can separate mixtures in several ways.

1 _____

Some mixtures, such as gravel and water, can be separated by **sieving**.
Substances with smaller particles, such as sand, can be separated by **filtration**.
Magnetic substances can be taken out using a **magnet** and substances that
dissolve can be separated using **evaporation**.

Make up this mixture and try separating its parts in different ways.

You will need:

a bowl
gravel
salt
water
paper clips
a magnet
a sieve

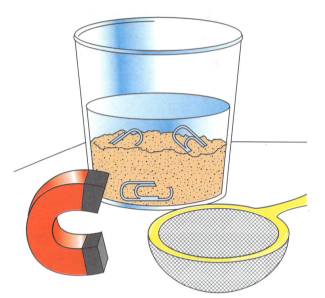

Mix up the gravel, salt, water and paper clips.
Take out the paper clips with the magnet.
Sieve the mixture to take out the gravel.
Put the salty water somewhere sunny and warm.
The water will evaporate, leaving the salt behind.

2 _____

What are the best ways to separate these mixtures?
Tick the best method.

Mixture	Sieving	Filtration	Evaporation
Rice and flour			
Sugar and water			
Tea leaves and water			
Gravel and sand			
Chalk and water			
Sand and water			

You could check your answers by trying to separate these mixtures yourself.

3

You can separate some solids from liquids by evaporation.

You will need:

sand
water
a plastic beaker
sugar

a Mix the sand and water in the beaker. Record below what happens to the mixture.

....

....

....

Does the sand dissolve in the water to produce a solution?

....

How could you separate the sand and the water?

....

b Mix some sugar and water in a beaker. Record below what happens to the mixture.

....

....

....

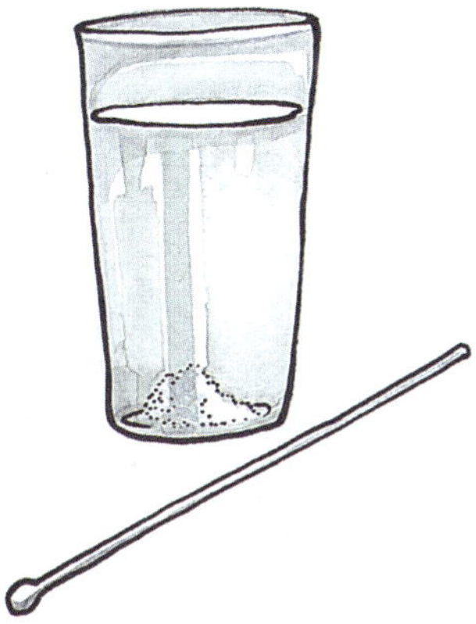

Does the sugar dissolve in the water to produce a solution?

....

How could you separate the liquid and the solid?

....

Now turn over ➤

21

Now try these ...

You can separate colours using **chromatography**.

1   Try separating the colours in felt tip pens.

You will need:
blotting paper
felt tip pens (water based)
water
a dish

Draw a spot of each colour about 1cm from
the bottom of the blotting paper.
Dip the bottom of the blotting paper into a dish
of water, making sure the water does not touch
the spots of colour.
Let the water soak up the paper.

What happens to the spots of colour? ....

Which ones are made up of more than one colour? ....

2   Now try separating the colours in food dye.

You will need:
blotting paper, cut into circles
a yoghurt pot
water
different coloured food dyes

Make two cuts in a circle of blotting paper
and bend the strip into a pot of water.
Put a drop of dye in the middle of the circle.
As the water is absorbed by the paper it will
dissolve the dye.
Rings of colour will form as the dye splits
into its parts.
Try this with other colours of dye.

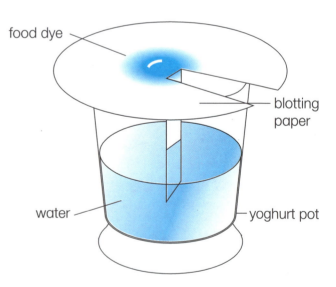

food dye

blotting
paper

water

yoghurt pot

More ways to help your child:

Try separating the ingredients in muesli by blowing on them. Relate this process to
the way grain is separated from chaff.

Try separating natural pigments by chromatography. Crush up leaves and orange and
yellow flowers in a few drops of water. Put a drop of the resulting greenish liquid on
some blotting paper. The colours should separate as the drop spreads out.

Bright or dim?

Introduction:

This Unit looks at increasing and decreasing the current in a circuit by varying the number of batteries or components, so making bulbs brighter or dimmer. Components can be wired up in a circuit in series or in parallel. In a **series** circuit, the components are linked together from battery to bulb to bulb and the current is shared between all the bulbs. In a **parallel** circuit each circuit receives the full amount of current from the battery and does not share it between the bulbs. A **resistor** is a component used to reduce the amount of current flowing in a circuit. The longer and thinner a wire is, the higher the resistance it offers, so coils of thin wire are often used in circuits to reduce the current. Variable resistors, whose resistance can be altered, are used in dimmer switches to control the light from a bulb. As the switch is turned, the length of wire between two contacts increases, so its resistance increases and the bulb dims.

National Curriculum:

Attainment Target 4: Physical Processes

At Key Stage 2 children are taught:

> *ways of varying the current in a circuit to make bulbs dimmer or brighter;*
> *and how to represent series circuits by drawings and diagrams.*

At Level 4 children should be able to explain how a particular device in an electrical circuit may be switched on and off. At Level 5 they should begin to apply ideas about physical processes to suggest a variety of ways to make changes, such as altering the current in a circuit.

Activity:

The first activity investigates what happens when you alter the number of batteries and the number of torch bulbs in a series circuit. The second activity asks children to construct a parallel circuit. When carrying out this activity, remind children of the previous activity so that they can compare the brightness of the bulbs. The final activity looks at resistors and children are asked to describe how a variable resistor might be used in two different circumstances. The activities on the 'Now try these' page look at internationally recognised symbols commonly used in circuit diagrams.

Teaching points:

Before your child attempts the first two activities look at the circuits together and discuss how they are set up. Encourage your child to make predictions about what will happen before trying out the activities. Remind your child about the concept of a complete circuit and the consequences of not having one. Go over vocabulary which can be used to describe the brightness of a bulb, for example dim, dull, bright, brighter and very bright.

The current and voltage used in these circuits is small but make sure your child is aware of the dangers of other batteries and electrical household appliances.

When the switches are constructed check that the connections are secure, otherwise the switch may not work properly.

Bright or dim?

How can we make lights brighter or dimmer?

1 _____

Here is one way to investigate changing the brightness or dimness of a bulb.

You will need:

three batteries
three torch bulbs and bulb holders
four wires

Make a simple circuit using two wires, a battery and a bulb.

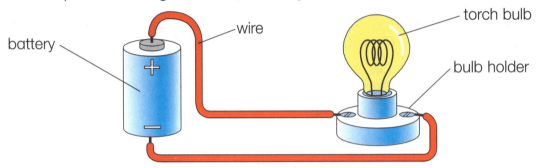

Now add a second battery. What happens to the bulb? ....

Now add a third battery. What happens to the bulb? ....

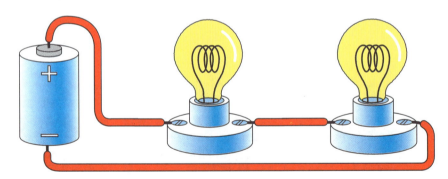

What happens if you add a second bulb to your circuit?

....

Try altering the number of batteries and bulbs. On a separate piece of paper, record your results in a table like the one below.

Number of batteries	Number of bulbs	Brightness of bulbs
1	1	Bright
2	1	Very bright

2 ————————

If one of the lights in your circuit is broken, what will happen to the others?
Tick the right box.

They will all light up except the broken one. ☐

None of them will light up. ☐

Do you know why? ....

3 ————————

Here is a different type of circuit you can make to change the brightness of your bulbs.

Make two circuits with one battery as shown below.

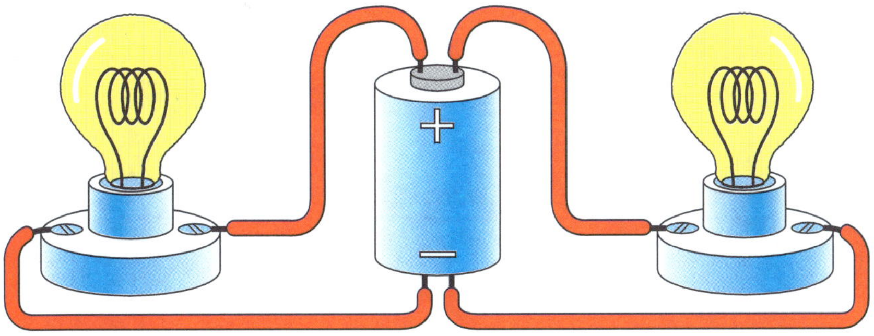

Are the two bulbs as bright as when there was only one bulb? ....

4 ————————

Resistors (components that stop electricity from flowing freely) are put into circuits to reduce the amount of current. Variable resistors can increase or decrease resistance. They are used in volume controls for stereos or in dimmer switches for lights.

How could a resistor be used in these situations?

a On a control unit for a toy car.

....

....

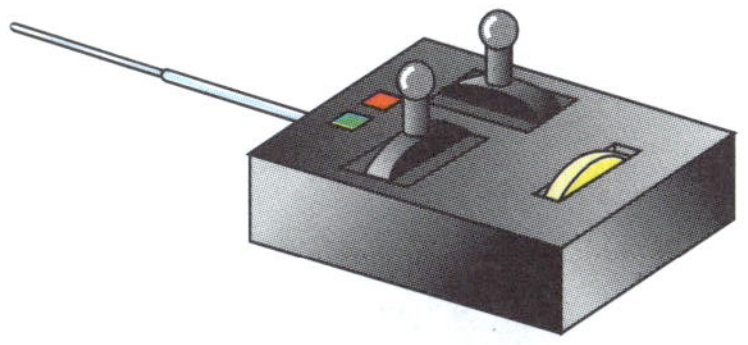

b On a radio.

....

....

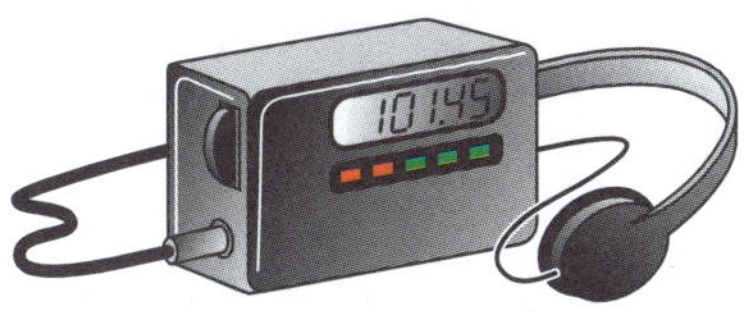

Now turn over ➤

Now try these ...

The symbols below are often used to draw a diagram of an electrical circuit.

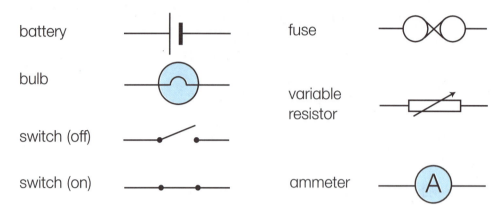

battery

fuse

bulb

variable resistor

switch (off)

switch (on)

ammeter

1 Can you fill in the spaces in this circuit by naming the symbols?

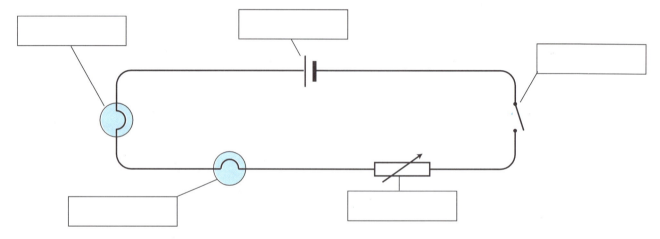

2 Look at the diagram below. Is the bulb in this circuit off or on? ....

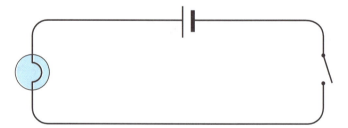

More ways to help your child:

Your child could make simple switches from paper clips and drawing pins (see Learning Workbook Science 8–9) to add to the circuits. He or she could then investigate which lights go out when the switches are off and on.

Get your child to build simple circuits and then ask him or her to draw the circuit using the symbols. You can also draw the symbols on pieces of paper and cut them out for your child to construct paper 'circuits'.

Taking care

Introduction:

This Unit encourages children to look after their bodies and treat them with care. It aims to help them realise the importance of exercise, a sensible diet and personal hygiene, and to be aware of the effects of smoking, alcohol and drugs. It is important that children are able to distinguish between drugs that are medicines and those that are harmful to the body.

National Curriculum:

Attainment Target 2: Life Processes and Living Things

At Key Stage 2 children are taught:

that tobacco, alcohol and other drugs can have harmful effects.

At Level 4 children should recognise that different organ systems carry out different life processes. At Level 5 children are expected to be able to explain the main function of some organs and the effects that smoking, drinking and drugs can have on the body.

Activity:

The first activity asks children to run around or do other physical exercise, like skipping or jumping, for about 10 minutes. They are then asked to list changes that have occurred in their body, for example an increase in their heartbeat, sweating or being out of breath. The next activity asks children to suggest a variety of exercises that people carry out to keep healthy. The third activity looks at what makes up a healthy diet while the final activity suggests some simple, 10-minute exercises that children can do to keep healthy. The follow up activity on the 'Now try these' page asks children to list some of the ways smoking, alcohol and medicine can affect the body. When working through this section, discuss the differences between drugs that help (medicines) and those that can damage the body.

Teaching points:

Your child could make some posters to encourage people to eat and drink healthily or to give up smoking. Your child could also conduct a survey of people's opinions about smoking or of the amount of exercise they take. Ask your local authority or doctor's surgery for further information on health issues.

Children with medical problems or who have had a recent illness or are taking medication should not take part in strenuous activity.

The fitter a person is, the quicker his or her pulse rate returns to normal after taking exercise. Your child could take his or her pulse rate before and after exercise and find out how long it takes to return to its resting rate.

Taking care

You must look after your body if you want to stay healthy.

1 _____

Taking care of your lungs, being sensible about what you eat and drink and keeping clean are all ways to keep your body healthy. You should also try to get lots of exercise.

Run around quickly, skip or jump for 10 minutes. Look at the ways in which your body has changed. Are you out of breath, for example? List the changes below.

a ....

b ....

c ....

d ....

2 _____

What kinds of exercise do people take to keep fit? Write some down.

a ....

b ....

c ....

d ....

Which do you think is the best exercise to take? ....

Why? ....

3

Circle the foods and drinks that will help you to keep healthy.

Which of these foods is best for your teeth? ....

Try drawing your own 'Healthy Food' poster.

4

Try these exercises every day to make your body more healthy.

Warm up by walking on the spot, pressing each foot in turn toe to heel. Start slowly and speed up to a gentle jog finally lifting your knees up in front. Keep jogging and then make loose fists and punch upwards and in front – first with alternate arms and then both together. Keep going until you are beginning to puff a bit for about 10 minutes.

Run or jump and hop forward and back and side to side. If you are with friends make up a country dance with star figures, chains and back to backs. Add hand claps.

Try jumping jacks – four little jumps feet together with arms above the head, four little jumps feet and arms apart, then two of each, then one of each.

Or try can can kicks – bounce with your feet together then kick up the right leg. Bounce with your feet together and kick up the left leg.

Don't forget to stretch out your muscles when you have finished exercising. Do side and back stretches and stretch out your legs on the ground.

Now turn over ➤

Now try these ...

How may the following things affect your body?

Smoking

a ....

b ....

c ....

d ....

Alcohol

a ....

b ....

c ....

d ....

Medicines

a ....

b ....

c ....

d ....

More ways to help your child:

Discuss why your child should look after his or her body. Make a list of things he or she can do to keep fit. Make a list of foods and look at the way each one is used by the body.

Get your child to look inside his or her mouth using a bathroom mirror and a dental mirror. How many teeth have fillings? Are any teeth missing? Can your child explain why his or her teeth are like this?

Drawing conclusions

Introduction:

Using information based on an experiment, children need to ask themselves why certain things happen and draw conclusions from their findings. They should know how to carry out fair tests, choose the right equipment for an experiment and draw their own conclusions from a set of results collected by others.

National Curriculum:

Attainment Target 1: Experimental and Investigative Science

At Key Stage 2 children are taught:

*to make comparisons and identify trends or patterns in results;
to use results to draw conclusions; and to indicate whether the evidence
collected supports any predictions made.*

At Level 4 children should, where appropriate, make predictions. They should make a series of observations and measurements and present these using tables and charts. They should begin to plot points to form simple graphs and use these graphs to point out and interpret patterns or trends in their data. At Level 5 children should be able to record observations and measurements systematically, draw conclusions that are consistent with the evidence and relate these to their scientific knowledge.

Activity:

The first activity asks children to investigate which materials make the best thermal insulators, and then to fill in a table of results. (To carry out this activity children will need a kitchen thermometer.) They are then asked to draw some conclusions from their experiment. Children should be encouraged to predict what will happen before they carry out the test, and to make sure that the test is fair. The second activity asks children to study a pie chart produced from someone else's results and to draw conclusions based on the results. The activity on the 'Now try these' page encourages children to use some collected data to answer questions about the strength of different materials.

Teaching points:

Attainment Target 1 does not contain any facts to be learnt, but aims to develop your child's skills of investigation and exploration – skills which are important in Science.

Encourage your child to make predictions, record results and draw conclusions. Not all your child's experiments will be successful, so encourage him or her to carry out experiments more than once if he or she feels that they are unfair.

Encourage your child to invent his or her own investigations. Make sure that he or she checks each activity carefully and records the results accurately.

Drawing conclusions

When you carry out an investigation, you should predict what will happen and record your results carefully.

1

Here is a simple experiment investigating **insulation**.

You will need:

empty drinks cans
hot water
Plasticine
tin foil
a woollen scarf
a sheet of newspaper
a cotton tea towel
a kitchen thermometer

ADULT HELP NEEDED

Wrap each can in a different material – tin foil, wool, newspaper and cotton. Ask an adult to heat up some water and pour hot water into each can. Take the temperature of the water in each can and record your results in the table below. Seal the cans with Plasticine. Wait five minutes, then take the temperature again. Take it again after another five minutes. Record your results in the table.

Material	Start temperature (°C)	5 minutes later (°C)	10 minutes later (°C)
Tin foil			
Wool			
Newspaper			
Cotton			

Which was the best form of insulation? ....

Do you know why? ....

....

What material had the greatest drop in temperature? ....

Why did this happen? ....

Would it make any difference if you used a container made from a different material?

Explain why...

2 ═══════════════════

This pie chart shows the different materials used to build a school.

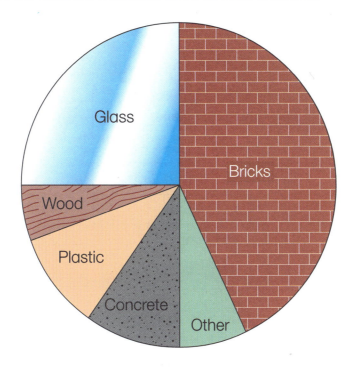

a Which was the most common material used?

....

b Why do you think so much glass was used?

....

c What do you think the concrete might have been used for?

....

d Do you think this school was built in this century? Explain why.

....

....

e What other materials might have been used to build the school?

....

Now turn over ➤

Now try these ...

Hannah and Ben decide to investigate the strength of different materials.
They hang weights on the end of each material until it breaks.

Here are their results:

Material	Weight added before material broke
Cardboard	500 grams
Newspaper	350 grams
Tissue paper	200 grams
Cotton	750 grams
Plastic	475 grams

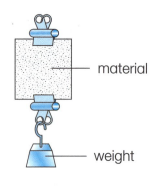

1   Which was the strongest material? Explain why.

....

....

2   Why do you think the tissue paper gave way so easily?

....

....

3   What kind of checks would you need to make sure that the experiment was fair?

....

....

4   Which would be the best material for making carrier bags? Why?

....

....

More ways to help your child:

Ask your child to record his or her pulse rate at half-hour intervals during the day.
Produce a line graph showing the results. What conclusions can your child draw from
the graph? For example: 'At 10 am, when my pulse was at its highest, I was playing football.'

Heave-ho

Introduction:

A force can make an object change its direction and speed. When an object is not moving, the forces acting on it are balanced, so the effect of a force in one direction is cancelled out by the effect of a force in the opposite direction.

National Curriculum:

Attainment Target 4: Physical Processes

At Key Stage 2 children are taught that:

forces act in particular directions; and that unbalanced forces can make things speed up, slow down and change direction.

At Level 4 children should be able to make generalisations about physical phenomena, such as motion being affected by forces, including gravity, magnetism and friction. At Level 5 they should begin to apply ideas about physical processes to suggest a variety of ways to make changes. At this level they should also begin to use some abstract ideas in descriptions, such as forces being balanced when an object is stationary.

Activity:

The activities in this Unit look at balanced and unbalanced forces. The first activity examines floating and sinking. When an object floats, balanced forces are acting on it. A table tennis ball floats in water, but a stone will sink. This is because the force of the stone downwards (due to gravity) is greater than the upthrust of the water. The forces are unbalanced and so the stone sinks. Children can see the upward force of the water by holding a large, light ball underwater and letting it go. The second activity goes on to look at how the shape of an object can affect its ability to float. Anything will float if the amount of water it displaces (pushes aside) weighs more than, or the same as, it does. The third activity looks at what happens in a tug of war with two people exerting forces on each other. The final activity is a forces game – blowing a table tennis ball like a football. This will give children a chance to investigate balanced and unbalanced forces independently. The activities on the 'Now try these' page look at the forces acting on a see-saw and how to balance them. A see-saw can be balanced even when one side has more weight on than the other, by placing the weights at different distances from the pivot. The simple formula: Distance from pivot x Weight will be equal for both sides of the see-saw. When trying out this activity, make sure the weights used are identical.

Teaching points:

Encourage your child to link forces with their effects, such as changes in shape, speed or direction of movement. Remind your child that gravity is the force that pulls objects downwards towards the Earth.

If you do not have a table tennis ball, use another hollow ball, such as an old tennis ball. Use a strong rope for the 'tug-of-war' activity. The football game should be played on a flat surface away from draughts. Use large drinking straws.

Heave-ho

If the forces working on an object are balanced, the object will stay still. If they are unbalanced, the object will change speed or direction.

1

Put a table tennis ball into a bowl of water. The ball does not sink,
because the force of gravity is balanced by the push back from the water.

Do the same thing with a stone instead of the ball.
What happens? Do you know why?

....

....

Make a collection of objects, for example: paper, coin,
orange, cork, paper clip, metal spoon.

Which do you think will float and which will sink?
Test your predictions and record your results in a table like this:

Object	Float or sink?	Was your guess right?
cork	float	yes

2

Whether an object floats or sinks depends on its shape, size and the material it is made of.

Put a large lump of Plasticine into a bowl of water. What happens?

....

Now model the lump of Plasticine into a boat
shape. What happens now?

....

Can you explain why this happens?

....

....

....

3

With a friend, pull on the ends of a rope. If you both use the same force, you will stay balanced. If one of you pulls harder, the forces will become unbalanced and the other person will move.

4

Have a game of **Blow Football**

You will need:

a table tennis ball
two large straws
goals made from card or straws
sticky tape
a large square of board or strong card
coloured paints

1 Paint the board or card to look like a football pitch and stick the goals to the ends.

2 Place the ball in the middle of the pitch.

3 You and a friend should stand at opposite ends of the pitch.

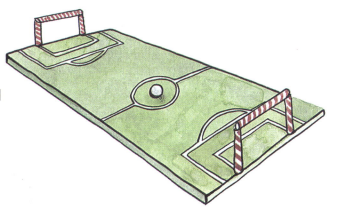

4 Blow through your straws and try to move the ball into each other's goal. The first one to score three goals is the winner.

When you both blow directly opposite each other with the same amount of force, the ball will not move. When the forces are not balanced, the ball will move or change direction.

Now turn over ➤

Now try these ...

Make a see-saw

You will need:

a 30cm ruler
some small weights
(you could use pennies)
a pencil

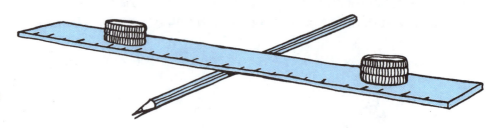

Balance the ruler on the pencil like a see-saw.
At what point does it balance? This is called the **pivot**.

Put a weight on one end of the ruler and another weight at the other end.
Make the see-saw balance. Now move one weight nearer to the pivot.
What do you have to do to the other weight to make the see-saw balance?

Put several weights on top of each other on one end of the see-saw.
What do you have to do to the other end to make it balance?

Now measure the distance from the weights each side to the pivot.
Multiply each length by the weight of the pennies on that side.
What do you notice?

How many ways can you make a real see-saw balance?

More ways to help your child:

Try floating objects in salt water. Salt water is denser than tap water and gives a stronger
upthrust. The more concentrated the salt water, the higher materials such as wood will float.

Your child could try constructing towers with building bricks or with paper rolled into
tubes and straws. If the forces balance the tower will stay up; if they don't it will collapse.
How high can your child build the tower? Is it strong enough to support a ball on top?
Can your child think of ways of strengthening the tower? Try constructing bridges in the same way.

Once in a lifetime

Introduction:

This Unit looks at the life cycles of human beings and other creatures. Different creatures have different patterns of growth. Children start to mature into adults at about 10–14 years of age for girls and about 12–15 for boys. Our bodies change to prepare for having children. As we reach old age, our muscles get weaker and our bones become more brittle. The cells in our bodies take longer to repair themselves and to replace any damaged parts.

National Curriculum:

Attainment Target 2: Life Processes and Living Things

At Key Stage 2 children are taught about:

the main stages of the human life cycle.

At Level 4 children recognise that different organ systems in animals and plants carry out different life processes. At Level 5 children should be able to describe the main stages in the life cycles of humans and flowering plants and point out similarities.

Activity:

The first activity investigates how our bodies change as we get older. The second asks children to put the main stages of growth in order. You can use this as a starting point to discuss the changes that take place in the body. The third activity asks children to find out some facts and figures about themselves as babies then compare them with their bodies now. They also have to think about how it might feel to be at different stages of the life cycle.The fourth activity asks children to draw their own lifeline, listing some of the main things that have happened to them. The activities on the 'Now try these' page ask children to put the life cycles of certain creatures in order and then compare the life cycle of a frog with that of a human. You could discuss the similarities and differences between the animal life cycles shown and that of a human.

Teaching points:

Many animals produce young that are very similar to themselves, but some produce very different offspring. For example, a moth will produce a caterpillar which will eventually change into a moth, but a snail will produce a tiny copy of itself.

Ask your child to produce an information chart including his or her height, weight, arm length etc. New sheets can be added every so often so that your child can see how his or her body is changing over a period of time. You could include a photograph with each sheet. Collect together some photographs of older members of your family as they are now and when they were children and babies, and make up a family gallery of photographs.

Once in a lifetime

As living things get older, they change.

1 _____

People change from babies into children, then to teenagers and into adults. By the time someone is 20 years-old, their body should be fully grown. Different parts of our bodies change as we grow older.

Look at the drawings below. How has this person changed as he has got older?

....

....

....

2 _____

Put these stages of the human life cycle into order below.

birth   fertilisation   teenager   death   child   old age   adult

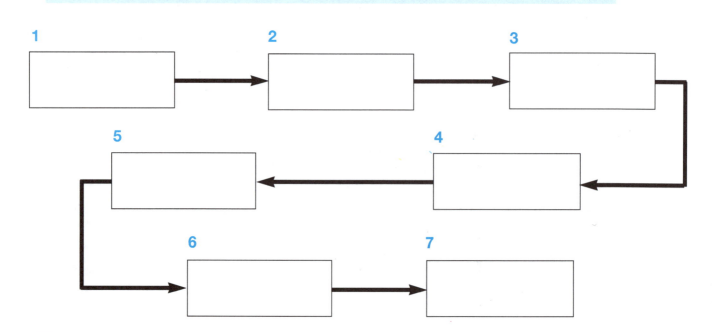

3

How have you changed since you were a baby?

Find some photographs of yourself and see if you can find out what you were like when you were born. Fill in the record chart below.

My:	At birth	Now
weight		
hair colour		
eye colour		
height		

a   What do you think it felt like to be a baby?

....

....

b   What do you think will happen to your body over the next ten years?

....

....

c   What do you think it will feel like to be a senior citizen?

....

....

4

Draw your own lifeline

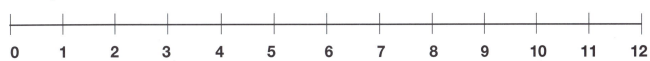

0   1   2   3   4   5   6   7   8   9   10   11   12

Write each year of your life on a chart, then note down some of the most important things that have happened to you since you were born. You could use pictures or words.

Make up some lifelines for other members of your family.

Now turn over ➤

Now try these ...

1   Put the life cycle of these creatures in the correct order by numbering them 1 to 4.

2   Look at the different stages in the life of a frog. How are they different to a human life cycle? Write your answer on a separate piece of paper.

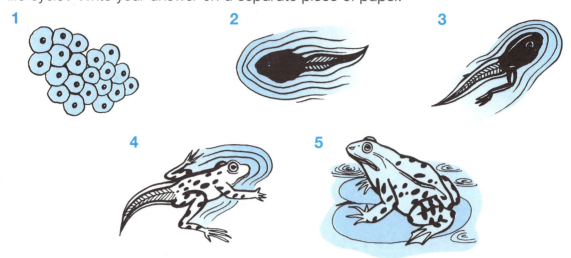

More ways to help your child:

Get your child to choose another animal and produce a lifeline. Compare this with the lifeline of a human. What are the similarities and the differences?

Lines of light

Introduction:

Light travels in straight lines so it cannot go around obstacles in its path. This is why shadows form. We are able to see objects because light bounces off them into our eyes. Shiny materials, such as polished metal, have smooth surfaces which reflect light in a regular way, producing a reflection. Flat shiny objects, such as mirrors, produce a sharp image. The direction of light can be changed by using objects such as mirrors.

National Curriculum:

Attainment Target 4: Physical Processes

At Key Stage 2 children are taught that:

*light is reflected from surfaces; and that we see light sources
because light from them enters our eyes.*

At Level 4 children describe and explain physical phenomena such as the idea of light travelling. At Level 5 children begin to use some abstract ideas in descriptions, such as objects being seen when light from them enters the eye.

Activity:

The first activity gives instructions for making a simple light box. This makes a single beam of light which can be used in a darkened room to see how light is reflected in a regular way by mirrors, but is scattered by irregular surfaces such as tin foil. The second activity looks at the law of reflections – that the angle at which light hits a mirror (the incident or incoming ray) is equal to the angle that light leaves the mirror (the reflected ray). If the light box is placed at a right angle to the mirror, the incident ray is shone straight back so no reflected beam is seen. The third activity explains how light reflects off things into our eyes – this explains why we cannot see anything in the dark. The activity on the 'Now try these' page gives instructions for making a simple periscope. It works because the light rays are reflected at the same angle as they come into the top mirror downwards to the bottom mirror and into the eyes.

Teaching points:

Your child will probably need some assistance in setting up the light beam box and making the periscope.

Discuss with your child how light usually travels in straight lines and is reflected in a predictable way by mirrors and other shiny surfaces.

Lines of light

Light travels in straight lines. It cannot go round corners on its own.

1

Make a light beam box

You will need:

an empty shoe box
scissors
a torch bulb and bulb holder
a battery
two wires
strong sticky tape

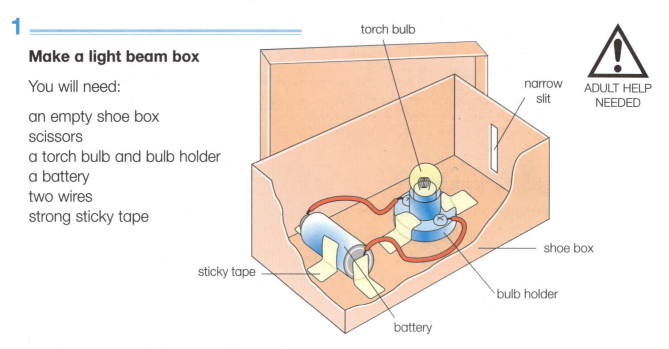

torch bulb

narrow
slit

ADULT HELP
NEEDED

shoe box

bulb holder

sticky tape

battery

1 Cut a narrow slit in one end of the box.

2 Wire the bulb and bulb holder to the battery and use sticky tape to fix the circuit inside the box.

3 Put the lid on the box.

Use your light beam in a darkened room. Shine the beam onto a mirror. Move the mirror and see if you can change the direction of the beam.

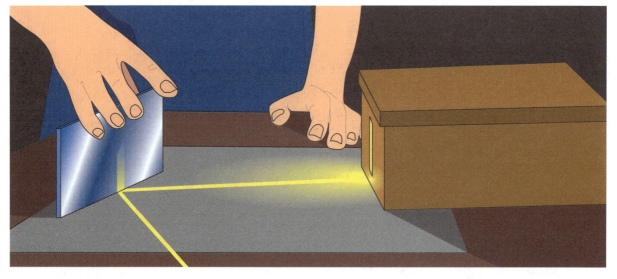

Can you reflect the light round a corner?
Try out other surfaces that reflect light, such as tin foil. What happens now?

You might like to record your observations on a separate sheet of paper.

2

Try this investigation in a darkened room to see how light is reflected.

You will need:

a light beam box
a mirror
white paper
pencils
a protractor

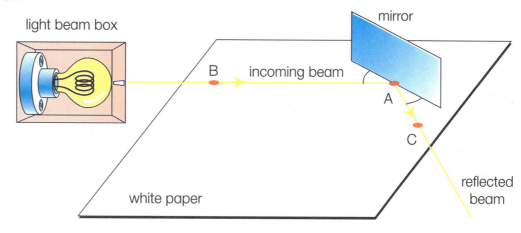

Set up your light beam box and the mirror as shown.
Draw a line along the length of the mirror and mark where the
beam hits the mirror (**A**). Now mark the incoming beam (**B**) and the reflected beam (**C**).
Remove the mirror and join up the marks with straight lines.
Measure the angle between the mirror and the incoming beam, and the angle between the
mirror and the reflected beam.

Are they the same? ....

3

Light travels to our eyes in straight lines.
We can see things because light bounces off objects straight into our eyes.

Why can't we see in the dark?

....

Now turn over ➤

Now try these ...

Make a simple periscope

You will need:

stiff card
scissors
a protractor
two mirror tiles about 12cm long
glue and sticky tape

Cut and fold the card as shown.
Stick the edges together.

**ADULT HELP
NEEDED**

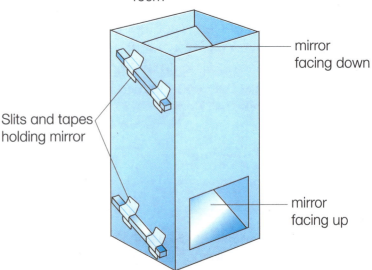

Now slide the two mirrors into the slots.
Use sticky tape to hold them in place.
Make sure the top mirror is facing
downwards and the bottom mirror
upwards.

mirror
facing down

Slits and tapes
holding mirror

mirror
facing up

Use your periscope to look over a high fence or a wall, or round a corner. How does it work?

....

....

More ways to help your child:

Play 'target practice'. Make a numbered target and put it up on a wall. Hold a mirror so
that it points in the general direction of the target. With a torch, your child should stand
about 2 metres from the mirror, then switch on the torch and see where the light hits the
target. Your child could re-adjust the position of the mirror until he or she hits a bull's-eye.

Your child could experiment with how the pupils of the eyes expand and contract in dim and
bright light. This is to control the amount of light that enters the eye.

page 5

1   a   veins arteries
      b   four
      c   300g
      d   lungs
      e   fist

page 6

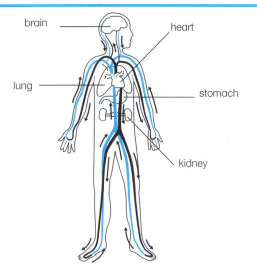

brain   heart   lung   stomach   kidney

page 12

1   The shadow should be shortest at midday.

pages 16–17

1   a   seagull
      b   crab
      c   periwinkle
      d   curlew

2   a   butterfly
      b   ladybird
      c   fly
      d   spider
      e   woodlouse
      f   snail
      g   worm

page 18

1   For example:
      a   Dogs are mammals: they are warm blooded, bear live young and have hair.
      b   Lizards are cold blooded, lay eggs and have a dry skin.
      c   A thrush is a bird: it is warm blooded, lays eggs and is covered in feathers.

2   R M R B
      M R B B
      R B MM

pages 20–21

2   sieving
      evaporation
      sieving
      sieving
      filtration
      filtration

3   a   The sand will not dissolve.
         It can be separated by filtration.
      b   Yes, the sugar does dissolve.
         It can be separated by evaporation.

page 22

The felt tip pens and food dye should spread out into bands of different colours.

pages 24–25

1   The bulb will get brighter with two and then three batteries.

    With a second bulb, the two bulbs will be dimmer than the single bulb.

2   None of them will light up.

    The circuit has been broken.

3   Yes.

4   For example:
      a   In the speed control.
      b   As part of the volume control.

page 26

1   a   battery
      b   bulb
      c   bulb
      d   variable resistor
      e   switch (off)

  2   Off

pages 28–29

1   For example: sweating, heart beat increases, out of breath.

2   For example: jogging, walking, cycling, gardening.

3   oranges, water, bread, fish, tomatoes, milk.
    Milk is good for your teeth.

page 30

For example:
Smoking can make you cough or short of breath.
Alcohol can make you careless or slow you down.
Medicines can help cure a headache or ease a sore throat.

pages 32–33

1   Wool will probably be the best insulator because it is thicker and traps more air.
    Using a different container will make a difference to the results because the container may be a better or worse insulator.

2   a   brick.
      b   For example: because schools need a lot of light.
      c   For example: to make paths and for the foundations.
      d   The school was built this century because plastic is included as one of the materials used.

page 34

1   Cotton, because it took the most weight before it broke.

2   Because it is much weaker than the other materials.

3   For example: each sample of material should be the same size; the weights must be added in the same way each time; the test should be carried out in exactly the same way for each material.

4   For example: plastic, because it is strong, waterproof and stretchy.

page 36

1   The stone sinks to the bottom, because the forces are unbalanced.

2   The Plasticine boat should float, because its shape allows it to displace (push aside) its own weight of water.

page 38

To make the see-saw balance the weights should be the same distance from the pivot.

If you move one weight closer to the pivot, the other weight must be moved further away.

With several weights at one end, the weight at the other end must be further away from the pivot to make it balance.

The numbers balance. The weight times the length on one side of the ruler will give the same answer as the weight times the length on the other side of the ruler.

page 40

1 For example: As people become older their skin becomes wrinkled and their hair turns grey.

2 1 fertilisation, 2 birth, 3 child, 4 teenager, 5 adult, 6 old age, 7 death

page 42

1   a d, c, b, a
    b d, c, a, b
    c c, d, a, b

2 For example: The egg and tadpole develop in water rather than inside the mother; a tadpole looks nothing like an adult frog; a frog's life is much shorter.

page 45

2 Yes, the angles should be the same.

3 We can't see in the dark because there is no light to bounce off objects.

page 46

The periscope works because light travels in through the top of the periscope. It is reflected off the top mirror and down the tube to the bottom mirror, where its reflected into the eye.